The Body Speaks...

HEALING THROUGH KNOWLEDGE

Dr. Vandana Gupta

Healing Center

Opposite Felicity, Near Mango Hill,
Bommayarpalayam, Tamil Nadu, India 605104
Ph. 91-413-2623494, +91 9655541134
Email chvandanaa@gmail.com
www.healingcentrevandana.wordpress.com

First Edition: 2009

Revised 2nd Edition: 2016

ISBN: 978-81-7060-284-2

Published by Healing Center, Bommayarpalayam, Tamil Nadu.

Printed in India

Contents

Foreword

Several years ago, when I had hurt my shoulder, a friend of mine suggested that I go see Dr. Vandana. I wasn't sure what to expect, but had faith in my friend and so I went. That started me off on such an interesting journey that very shortly afterwards, even though bringing the shoulder back to normal was a painful journey that took a significant amount of time, I was always grateful that I had hurt it, since it had led me to such interesting insights into life itself, and mine in particular. Through her I was able to see the ephemerality of illnesses or limitations of the body. I knew that the Mother and Sri Aurobindo had spoken of this, but it was not my experience. Vandana helped me actually experience the truth of it in myself and perhaps even more profoundly in my nephew Michael who came to visit me shortly after having been diagnosed with an 'incurable disease'. When he was coming, I told Vandana about the diagnosis and she gave a little laugh, because to her nothing was incurable. Indeed, with her help, he was able to alter his condition so that it is now not a problem in his life.

This is how he describes his experience with the auto-immune disease called colitis.

"I do attribute my work with Vandana as a great contributor to my healing path. In fact, she was the first doctor I went to who said I didn't have to live with the disease. That was where the first seed of healing was planted. And in the process, she also gave me the great gift of shifting how I relate to suffering in general. She taught me how deepening my relationship to powers greater than myself can be an important component to one's physical health and conversely that the imbalances in one's health can be a wonderful invitation to broaden one's commitment to a spiritual practice. A lot of our guided sessions were spent mindfully 'dropping down' into the parts of my body that were affected most, which was from my stomach to the base of my spine. Both the verbal and non-verbal exchanges during those sessions were palpable steps to feeling better physically and feeling an overall confidence that the healing would be progressively more penetrating.

I also found Vandana's process with my illness was the best way to experience surrender and detachment, which are very important spiritual tools, but were just concepts and ideals that were hard to grasp before that experience. The spiritual tools that Vandana helped me grasp are innumerable to list, but they included faith, devotion, mindfulness, patience, self-love, acceptance, compassion, and gratitude. I found her confidence very genuine and her investigative approach informed and with purpose. Her tone also was full of compassion without losing directness and bluntness when it was necessary.

Working with Vandana and my illness was an experience

that I have never taken for granted and it has blossomed into greater meaning over the years. It started with getting my health back, but it has led to a much greater spiritual health than I could have ever achieved on my own. Both the illness and the doctor were great boons on that part of my life's path. Vandana helped me embark on a greater journey than just feeling better physically. As Vandana said, 'When your health improves, then like-minded people will appear,' and she was right. The 'sangha' as the Buddhists call it, or the fellowship component to a spiritual life, which I was also seeking at that time, was an important puzzle piece to fall into place, and the blessing of now having a wonderful wife, friends and professional community has solidified my health and imbued the world with meaning and beauty."

My nephew's experience was one of many instances of Vandana's help. I myself continue to work with Vandana because every session brings new insights of various kinds and helps me be more in touch with what I consider my true self. This book she has written now enables others to see and experiment with the kind of journey that has helped me and many others. Through it, one could start out on one's own, exploring the inner state through the feelings of the body which could lead to many insights into one's self and the outer world by following her methods and by extension, other methods including one's own discoveries. I highly recommend it.

Nancy Whitlow
(Teacher, International Centre of Education,
Sri Aurobindo Ashram, Pondicherry)

Background

We are human. The moment we entered this earth we became small, helpless, limited. In some way or the other, we are struggling against these odds to find a way of being happy, peaceful, secure, loved, powerful, knowledgeable and free. Through all life, consciously or unconsciously, we search for this. Strangely it is all the time within us.

THIS BOOK

This book is extracted from the work of people who healed themselves of physical illnesses. It is an example of what you could discover in your own process of healing.

It also gives the way to organize a practice session with yourself.

It has helped people find their way back to themselves when they were suffering from physical problems. All these people could cure themselves of physical illnesses. In the process, they also recovered their own light, truth and joy.

THE PREMISE

We are souls that have taken a body. We are a spark of That which created the universe. Through us, It lives and enjoys and continues to create this earth and life... but we live as if we are blind, ignorant, helpless and small. In fact all of life seems to be hammering the message that we are helpless and small. Yet something in us refuses to believe it. We continue to hope and love and enjoy life because deep inside us we know that we are not only the body, the emotions or sensations or the thoughts. I think—thinking happens in me... I love—the feeling of love takes place in me. I have a pain or a skin problem or a headache, I am not the pain or the skin problem or the headache... So this 'I' is different from the body which I call me. This 'I' can watch, smell, hear and feel. When it looks out it sees, hears, smells and feels the external world. When it turns its gaze into the inner spaces, it sees, hears, smells, feels things that are within and spaces that are not physical.

Due to this 'I', each person views and experiences the world differently. People call this a 'subjective' view. It is not as highly regarded as an 'objective' viewpoint. Yet it is as important as the objective view.

Also, the inner world can be as clear as the outer, even if it is different for each one of us and different at different moments in time. In fact every one lives in the same world differently, for no two people live or see events the same way! The world outside is only a reflection of the inner reality. The body reflects what is happening within. Emotions and thought patterns are also only a script generated by 'me'. In this way almost all illnesses reflect an inner process that 'I' am undergoing at this moment of my life.

When we fall sick, we are suffering inside.

One could use this time of illness to reconnect to the 'real' suffering. In this, way effortlessly the outer illness disappears!

THIS WAY

We use our inner senses to explore what is happening inside us without judgement. We do not do anything. We just look, feel, sense or listen to what is going on within. We suspend the thoughts of "how I should be" and just observe "how I am". We allow the inner worlds to reveal themselves through images or colours, sounds or sensations. These are our own. Even an absence of them is our personal way of being. We watch everything as it is without getting involved in it. A part of us experiences the problem or discord and a part is free, just watching. There is no molding of the 'bad scenes' or visualizing 'beautiful ones'. We just look at what is, accepting all—good or bad, happy or sad, ugly or beautiful, without getting involved. In a way it is like Vipassana, but unlike Vipassana, here our search is to go deeper into the depth of the problem and look at the roots, if we can. For when we can reach the root of the problem, physical or mental or emotional, a strange thing happens. It dissolves and is replaced by a light or peace or joy or love. You did nothing but look!

THE PROCESS

1. Rest comfortably. You should be able to remain in this position for about an hour.

2. Close your eyes.

3. Become alert, alive to all that is happening inside your body. For convenience, you can scan the body from head to toe. Feel, see, hear and sense each part as your awareness touches it.

4. With your awareness go through the whole body once before coming to the area that is in trouble. This area will want your attention. It may be in pain or feeling uneasy or weak...

5. If there is more than one spot that is not feeling well, select the one that is most unwell.

6. Explore this area with your awareness: its place; its dimension; how deep does it go; what is its quality, that is, is it heavy, is it like a block, like a hole, etc. Are there any emotions, thoughts or images that come up as you explore this area?

7. Speak aloud what you experience. This is very important.

You are speaking to the part that is suffering.

If your expression is true, the suffering disappears! If it is partially true there is a relief but not fully. You then need to continue your exploring. If it is only your imagination, nothing will happen physically. The problem will remain as it is. You then need to start the exploration again, speaking of it as it actually feels to you.

8. Please do not try to correct anything (e.g. if you experience anger do not say, "I should not be angry"; if you see a black pit just experience and express it as it is). The pure experience expressed relieves the problem.

9. In case nothing moves or changes still, try to understand what is creating this experience. Ask yourself: "What is creating this?" Then wait without thinking of the reason. Either a memory, emotion or something else will surface, which you again express simply. Maybe your attention is drawn to some other part which is the origin of the problem here.

10. As the problem resolves itself, it is replaced by peace, light, joy or a stillness. Experience this for a moment before opening the eyes.

11. One session may not be enough to fully resolve a problem if it is deep-seated. One needs to come back and go deeper within.

12. Sometimes a session may trigger dreams or memories. Please be aware of them without judgement or brooding over them. The awareness itself has the power to resolve suffering! There are untold treasures in the inner spaces. It is up to you to explore, to go where you have never been...

THESE SESSIONS

Based on the yoga of Sri Aurobindo and the Mother, we explored ways to connect to the witness self and thereby bring the inner light forward.

We started by being aware of the Mother's presence. The person was often sitting or lying down with the eyes closed. He/she then did a survey of the whole body—part by part—recording how each area felt or what colours or images came forward. Often no images or colours came, only sensations. These were spoken aloud. Then the whole body was sensed in the same manner, allowing the attention to go to the area that had the maximum discomfort. From this area, the person looked deeper into the inner subtle body, keeping an attitude of allowing things to surface without DOING anything to them. Everything was just seen with a detachment and, as far as possible, total awareness.

Every one of us has an inner perception. The acknowledgement of whatever we perceive without judgement is the key to wellness.

TIME TAKEN

This varies from person to person. Each session can take about 30 to 45 minutes. A lot of time is also taken on sharing life events, the effect the inner work had on outer life situations and the dreams that emerged. The following sessions were of about 30 minutes to an hour each.

When it is the moment, a person's vision or perception can open into the karmic past and get to the roots of the problem there. Such sessions are not transcribed here as this is only an introduction to the process of healing through an inner knowledge.

Only a few sample sessions are presented here. They are selected to help you on your own inner journey.

The beginning

The inner work uses the body as a beginning. By feeling, sensing and looking at the different parts of the body, we are clearly, without doubt, led to the area in our self that is suffering!

This chapter is an example of how a session can begin.

S: I am doing this project on 'Divine Love'. So I started studying the works of the Mother and Sri Aurobindo, especially *Letters on Yoga*. I divided my work into the following topics: Human love, Divine love, Transformation of the nature. I got stuck at human love. Why is it that I find it difficult to communicate with people? I prayed to the Mother to teach me as to what I needed to do as a project. Fear gripped me for two hours. It was a terrible fear which gripped my entire body. So the Mother was showing me, "This is what is in you, this fear." So I started to do a project on fear. Since then I am studying fear. I also looked at the book *Integral Health*. Where I would need your help is if you can make me aware through the body consciousness: how can my body heal itself? I have hairfall, creating bald patches. It is getting better but it is never really okay. I also have dry scaly skin on the elbows and knees. I have done courses in Pranic healing*. I also used to have acidity but the stomach is now healthy. The only thing I now have is a skin problem.

V: How long?

S: 30 years... baldness for 30 years, the other is perhaps 10 years. I am using Ayurvedic medicine. The hair is growing very, very slowly. I don't know if it will ever completely heal or I have to keep taking medicines. Depression used to be my problem too, though I don't suffer from it any more. With Pranic healing it went. Negativity too I don't have any more. I do feel more love for me, confidence is there. My mind is freer definitely. And I want to get rid of this anxiety. It is still stuck there—this anxiety. This is very deep-rooted, since childhood I think... an anxiety in the mind. And in the vital there is a depression; in fact a fear is there. So how will you help me? What will you do?

V: Now is the time for an inner work.

S: And what about the physical illness?

V: The physical illness will also subside. You see, She has shown you that one of the main roots of your problems is fear. So this needs to be worked out.

S: The thing that is troubling me is the hair. Shall I show it to you?

V: Hmm...Yes, yes...

We look at the body's problem together.

* A method of energy healing taught by the late Master Choa Kuk Sui.

S: The physical problems are there; they are not going away. I am never free. They are always in my thoughts. But they are really in the body. They are not inside.

V: Yes, but root is anxiety and fear. The physical body only reflects what is happening inside. We can start the process together by looking inside. A part of you is feeling, connecting and experiencing what is happening in the body, the emotions or the thoughts and yet you are completely detached, watching it all. This is the key to the process. Nothing belongs to you; the fear or the anxiety or the events that happen...nothing. In nothing are you to be totally involved... you just watch... a part of you just looks at the thing, that's all. There is no action, nothing to change or to do, not to convert the vision to something you want, nothing like that. You just watch. And as you look, things themselves start changing, especially if you have the intention that you want to be well. You just watch the phenomenon and allow it to pass.

This is actually a work with the consciousness. When we are looking together, at a difficulty, be it a pain, a discomfort, a heaviness or an emptiness, we try to be as totally aware as possible. The awareness itself leads to a shift. This shift is to your 'true' self which radiates tranquillity, light, joy and peace. Once here, the physical problem dissolves and you are 'Well' in a real sense of wellness.

S: Yes, now I am free from most of the severe problems like headaches. But the urine problem is still there. I still have this increased frequency of urination.

V: This is again connected to anxiety—this and the hair-fall. If we can look at the anxiety through inner images... in fact this work is linked with images—colors, images, sensations. When we go into these areas (the head or the bladder) with our conscious awareness, we look for a feedback from within. We are starting a dialogue with the inner being. Wherever the consciousness goes, you look, you see, and then let it pass without holding on to any experience. You can see things as you would in dreams. If the clarity is there, you see them. We do not do anything, neither you nor I. We just watch.

S: I understand. I am very enthusiastic about it. I really want to overcome this through the Mother's force.

V: This is an inner work. It is a work with the inner being. It is one of the ways. What happens when you watch with detachment is that your *true self* takes over. There is the outer being where we have the problems. This undergoes a change as we connect to the inner self. Like you say, the fear gripped you. How did it pass? It passed because you were watching it.

S: I was sitting in front of the Mother's picture. So when I realized "Oh this is what I have to work on" and I knew that the Mother was showing it to me, I was no longer a victim of the fear, it was just a realization that this needs to be thrown out. So it was no longer a fear; that is what happened.

V: So it is this movement: not holding on to anything, not shrinking, not getting involved. A part of the being experiences the problem, a part of the being suffers, but another part is just watching. Then it changes.

S: Then will this have an impact on the physical?

V: We are going from the physical problem into the inner state connected to it. So it is *being* with the physical problem from inside. In your case you have already discovered that the root is in fear. So the way we will start is with the awareness of the fear and anxiety. It is this knot that has to open. As it opens, all the effects it has created on the physical body will dissolve.

S: Okay. So however long they may have lasted, it does not matter?

V: Yes. It is not a matter of time; it is a shift of consciousness. It is an inner shift that happens. Whether you are stationed in the outer being or the inner; it's a matter of where you are. So at this moment you can start by closing your eyes and observing the different parts of your body. How do they feel—the head, the neck, the shoulders. If there is a problem observe where it is exactly, what is its extent and how deep does it go.

S: Since morning I have been experiencing a problem. From the nape of the neck to the head, there is a pain. When I am quiet, the head collapses and shrinks.

I have come with a friend and she did something silly. You know in Pondicherry it has to be done differently. I could not say anything to her, because she might get upset. Yet I thought: What will the others say as she broke a rule here and there. So in my heart there was a conflict: If I tell her, will it hurt her? My mind just shut down. The whole thing though small was looming very large. I thought: What will others think of me if I don't tell her? The phenomenon is that my heart suffers as my mind just exaggerates things. Then it attracts all that I imagine and the wrong things happen.

So there is a pain here, in the heart, very intense...

V: Go into the pain. Feel the pain. See how deep it goes. Try to describe it.

S: The pain is very clear. I feel a pain; the pain is of what the other person is thinking about me. It is like I am containing it... like a bag... like a bag full of water that might at any time burst. Then what is happening is an irritation inside. I am trying to control myself. There is this huge anger against myself. I cannot do anything, so it is gathering. Yes, I feel it very clearly: anger, fear and an inability to do anything about the situation.

V: And when you look into the anger what happens?

S: It is like a movement starts in the heart.

V: All these movements, where do they start?

S: Well, here is the pain *(pointing to the chest)*.

V: Look inside this area and try to see the colours or the things happening there.

S: I see muscles contracting. I see blackish...

V: Do not tell me. Speak as if you are speaking to that part.

S: Okay, okay...

V: As you speak to the part, if you are speaking the true words, things change. So you are understanding and speaking to this part of yourself.

S: The muscles are clinging and holding on to something... there is something dark, very dark, purplish black... it is actually very angry...

V: Just be with the anger, feel the anger fully, try to go behind it. Don't remain with the event, but with the pattern that triggered this reaction. What triggered this reaction?

S: Fear of what the other person is thinking of me—fear and grief.

V: What creates the fear and grief?

S: A loss of perfection; that a perfect image must be maintained; that my image of perfection will be broken.

V: How do you feel now?

S: A great relief. There is a lightness coming inside me now. I can see a light in my heart.

V: Why must this 'image of perfection' be maintained?

S: Because my mother demanded it from me very severely... right from my childhood. I feel totally suffocated by it. I don't want it. I want to be natural, I want to be free.

V: What prevents you from being natural?

S: Feelings are coming out which I never acknowledged. I have the strength now. The faith, the fact that... you know I had to do things perfectly otherwise I would be reprimanded very severely. So a sort of clinging happened. I used to create an image of perfection. When that would break, it was like my identity would break. It was like a fear of getting exposed.

V: How do you feel when you acknowledge these feelings?

S: Freedom is coming... lightness... heaviness is going away, like a baggage...

V: Can you allow that image to leave?

S: I want to break that image... a little bit of relaxation... I don't have to grip. Today we have touched the core... really... the pain is gone! Really, it's really gone. I feel light, here *(showing the head)*. I feel light, in the back of the head.

V: One needs to be aware of the truth, however difficult it may be. The acknowledgement of the truth makes for a lightness. Within you is a light, a real way of being. The environment however teaches you to be different. When the environment and your truth are not in harmony, there is a conflict. These conflicts lead to a disharmony, an unwell-ness. We can actually fall sick or get deformed because we unconsciously cling to what others have taught us. We do not stand in ourselves. When we look inside with a full awareness, we stand in a free space and are empowered. The real freedom is to be in harmony within.

We exist on so many different levels. How can they all move together so that they don't jar? How can it become like good music? Good or bad it doesn't matter—just the awareness of so many notes coming together. We have so many levels, so many rhythms, so many resonances. What is the key to this music? The key is the truth of **your being** that is in tune with the universal truth and the tran-scendent truth. Because of the discordances in our life the notes get blurred. Our work will be to bring this harmony back. It is your work with yourself. I am only there to assist you, like a midwife one could say.

S: I will have a new birth! How wonderful!

V: We will start this together, but as time goes by you should be able to do this anywhere by yourself. Once you get the hang of it, it should be very simple.

END NOTE

This process continued for 35 sessions, which were spread over seven months. During this time, S went deeper into the areas she had identified in the course of these sessions; namely the hole at the navel and the samskaras. She went into images that seemed to come from memories of past lives. By looking at them she could shift into her true self where she felt vast, free, powerful and peaceful.

Her physical difficulties with the skin have almost gone. Her hair has started growing well. She is finding life deep and challenging. Her relation to her mother has shifted drastically. In fact, her mother has started healing herself. The fears and anxieties do not grip her as before. Every day has become a discovery of potentials.

For S, the way to connect to the inner world was through colours and images but the process is unique to each one of us. The inner journey is not predictable. Each of us has our own symbols, colours or no colour, sensation or sense experience. All of us DO have an inner world that we need to explore from time to time. All of us CAN do it at any time, in any place and in our own style. In fact, most of us go into this inner space at night or when we are quietly in nature without any disturbance.

The basis of this way is an attitude of acceptance of anything that we feel or sense without criticism or judgement. Then, as we turn our gaze within, many things—thoughts, feelings, sensations, colours and images—surface. Without getting too involved, we watch what rises and go deeper into the areas that call our attention. The aim is to try and SEE the root of the problem without trying to change it.

*"...we can, in this way, by an inner detachment, a mental or spiritual separateness, partially or even fundamentally liberate ourselves from the control of mind nature or vital nature over the being and assume the position of the witness, knower and ruler."**

This is one of the ways of healing ourselves without medicines.

* *Sri Aurobindo. The Life Divine. Pondicherry; Sri Aurobindo Ashram Trust, 1970, p.525.*

Discovering wounds

The body does speak. Its way of expression is often transmitted through sensations, vibrations or feelings. When we express what it is undergoing through words, sounds or images—very purely without frameworks of good or bad, right or wrong—there is a great relief! And if we can go deep enough to discover what creates this discomfort and speak to the body about our understanding, it can disappear forever.

It is interesting to realize how clearly the body responds to the truth. If you have a pain in the abdomen which is, say, caused by indigestion and you say to the body, "I understand that this is caused by anxiety" the pain will increase! Only when you relate it correctly to indigestion, will it disappear. If you are imagining some cause it will have no effect. TRUTH is the key.

Another important thing to note is that when you express something aloud, you must be truly CONNECTED to the body. Otherwise all is in your head, nothing will work.

This works for any physical or psychological problem reflected in the body. Two different cases in which this phenomenon was experienced first hand are given below.

FIRST CASE

J: I have a bend in the spine at the chest level since the age of 7 years. I am now 40 years old. I find it difficult to do some asanas. Otherwise it creates no problem. Do you think we could work on it?

V: Of course we can. Can you feel it clearly now, at this moment?

J: Yes, I can feel it clearly.

V: So what do you feel?

J: I feel a sort of tension there. The curve is pushing my chest outwards. Of course this gives a very good look for yoga postures but it is a little uncomfortable.

V: So should we start looking inside?

J: Yes.

V: What do you feel in the neck area?

J: A gripping...

V: Back of the neck?

J: No, actually the gripping is here, in the neck, where the neck joins the chest. It is as if the two parts of the body, the head and the chest, are separate from each other.

V: Then we come to the shoulders.

J: They are OK.

V: Then we come to the chest...

J: There are two extreme movements always happening in the chest. I realise something is not free. It is shrinking.

V: What's happening?

J: It is closed, held with strings... sinking...

V: So on the surface you feel a tension, while in the depths there is a sinking.

J: I am very happy usually. But now I see that something inside is not feeling well.

V: What are the colours you see in the chest?

J: A grey cloud.

V: Can you go deeper into this?

J: Yes, I am going into it.

(There is a deep silence as J is feeling and looking into the chest area. This space which he is in is a subtle, not physical space.)

As there is no response for a long while, V asks:

V: Can you put your hand there? Put your whole hand there and feel that area with your hand. Is it cold there or warm?

J: It is cold.

V: And what do you see?

J: It's too dark here...very black.

V: Go back to the time when this deformity started. So how does it feel? Is it painful, is it contracted or just normal?

J: It is very painful. *(He starts weeping silently.)* I can see clearly now. I have lost trust in my connection to the Divine. I must now analyze everything to understand the world.

V: How does the chest feel now?

J: Lighter. Much better. It seems as if the spine has changed. Could it be true?

We check the posture together. The curve is now normal.

J: Somehow this is too powerful. I have no control. I cannot believe that it could be so simple.

V: How do you feel in that area?

J: You know, it feels like I have become younger. I am free! A heavy burden has gone.

END NOTE

This session took half an hour. We have met a few times after this, but never for the back. For the last 10 years that I have known him, the back has been aligned and straight!

For me, this case was an eye-opener. Trained in allopathic medicine I never thought spinal deformities could be corrected without any physical manipulation.

It made me realise three things:

1. Consciousness is anterior to the physical form.

2. Our bodies are moulded by who we are.

3. The power of truth.

SECOND CASE

This is a story in which no doctor or witness helped. The person underwent the whole process herself, looking within to go deeper. Some people find this easier since they can then choose their own time and space.

I have been suffering from asthma since the age of 10 years. Since it runs in my family, no one was surprised. As my parents are doctors, I was given the regular medicines. But the frequency and severity of the attacks went on increasing. I too started studying medicine. In my final year, I had become so bad that I needed nebulization and drips. By the time I reached internship, I was on steroids. There seemed to be no hope.

I tried Homeopathy, Tibetan medicines and Ayurvedic medicines, with not much relief. Allopathic medicines helped but the side-effects left me shaken.

One day, when I was suffocating and could barely breathe, I decided to discover what was happening. I was then 27 years old.

I watched my chest moving fast. I felt the gasping for air. I felt the constriction of my chest. I heard the wheezing of the breath. I felt myself feeling totally helpless and alone.

I asked myself, "Why are you like this?"

There was blankness at first. As my need to understand was intense, a sort of quietness came.

I noticed that the breathing was better. The wheezing had decreased considerably.

Still I asked, "But why?"

I saw a big dark area, fully blocked, in the centre of my chest. It was heavy, dense and impenetrable. I could feel that the breathing was changing in response to this heavy, blocked thing. It was somehow creating the shortness of breath.

I asked, "What is this?"

I was flooded with an intense, deep pain. It was so bad that I could not even cry. I could only gasp in anguish.

Mentally, I could not understand. I had a happy childhood, with very loving parents. All my needs were gratified and more was given. There was no sorrow anywhere in my life apart from small hurts or pains. So what was this deep sorrow?

It was deep. It was old. It was as if I had lived with it for a long time. Then I remembered how I used to weep while going to school on my cycle when I was 10 years old, not knowing why I was crying.

So here it was: the unknown sorrow.

I asked, "Why are you suffering?"

Suddenly, the whole area became light. I was free! The breathing became normal. There was no wheezing anymore!

As I looked inside my chest, there was a space like a vast ocean without limits. This was filled with a soft, loving glow. There was a presence that was infinite in dimensions and sensing. It seemed to be my truth. At that moment I realized how I kept trying to adjust myself to the people around me, so that I could be like them and that I could feel what they feel and be as they were. Now I was me!

It was a revelation.

I opened my eyes. The place looked different. It was as if I had grown taller.

Since then (it is now 23 years), I have never had a really serious attack. I stopped regular medication totally. When I start getting breathless, I quiet myself down and go inside.

How lucky I am to have discovered this treasure!

END NOTE

1. It is interesting to see how we create disease when we move away from our truth. That is why Ayurveda calls a healthy person 'swasth', which means seated in him/her self.

2. It is also noteworthy that in this case and perhaps many others, unless the real cause of the problem is touched, the cure cannot happen. So even Ayurvedic, Homeopathic and Tibetan medicines could not help this person because the suffering was not physical but spiritual.

3. Allopathic medicine worked. Why? A belief in it perhaps, since both her parents and she herself were doctors. Or, were the bronchodilators stronger in Allopathy than other systems?

4. Her determination to get to the root cause was the trigger to the cure of years of suffering. Otherwise the process could have been terminated as her breathing became easier. This would have been a relief but not a radical effect as happened here.

5. Sometimes, people cannot get to the root. It is then wise to wait till the inner being is ready to reveal its secrets or till the intense urge to understand arrives.

Healing a problem by being there

By now we have discovered what it is to be aware. We have seen how awareness can dissolve a problem. The important thing is that one can stand before a problem inside oneself without shrinking. And just the fact that one can stand there with a deep awareness allows it to open up. Light can enter. Darkness can fade away.

This is a work in the inner domains. Theories do not help —experience can.

All the time people look at the smallness. Very rarely do we look at who we really are—what we truly are. It is understandable that we were born into a littleness but we were not always little. We are the soul that incarnated on earth. It is the discovery inside you of the power of the light and the dark. It is your process, your discovery. There is no analysis. The work of a healer is only to assist you in this discovery. Perhaps if you were alone there could be the tendency to repeat patterns without seeing them or dwelling too much at one point in the darkness... to go on focusing on the mud. A healer's role is to show you the step beyond. To discover it is yours...

Another important thing to remember is that the heavy or

dark stuff that we are looking at belongs to all of us. It is not only yours. You might have a special way of creation in the mud but each of us is in it. We build forms in it. We have our own fears, our own anxieties, our own ways of reacting. The light of the soul is also ever-present and eternal in all of us. As we stand in our truth we bring light into this mud. So the darkness and the heaviness have a possibility of growing towards this light. This is the difference between running away from the world and trying to transform the world. If you want to go away from the mud you can also do that, you can go only into the light. But on this way that we are walking, when your light connects to the mud, the mud starts changing.

Being strong enough to stand in the mud and understand its place, it is possible for the mud to open to the light. Everything in its right place is harmony, balance and health. Anything out of place or exaggerated is dis–ease.

The following is an excerpt from someone who regularly does this inner work to realign himself and get rid of any physical troubles that may have come. It is done with someone whom he trusts to give him the possibility to be free mentally and able to concentrate better and longer.

Q: So should we start now? We start by feeling Her Presence. At this moment look above your head. What do you see?

(Pause to allow for looking)

A: I see a dark cloud.

Q: Then, coming to the head...

A: A heaviness is there. This is especially dense on the left side. There is also a deep sharp pain in the centre of the brain.

Q: Then we come to the neck.

A: The neck is tight, like this (makes a fist) in the back, as if caught by a rope.

Q: Next we come to the chest.

A: Lot of unease and unnecessary activity.

Q: Back of the chest?

A: Pain...

Q: Then we come to the abdomen...

A: There is tightness in the solar plexus. It is there in the front more than the back. As I look I feel also a heavy pain at one point on the left side, in the front. It is circular in shape, like a hole, going very deep, almost into the middle of the abdomen.

Q: What is the type of pain?

A: It is like... whatever is clinging doesn't want to let go and... it is an emotional pain.

Q: Try and go into the hole if you can. See where it leads you. Go to the end. Just be open and accepting.

(after a pause)

So what is happening now?

A: It is widening now.

Q: As you go deeper into the hole what do you sense?

A: A connection to someone who is full of pain.

Q: Go still deeper... Just BE in front of it.

A It is a silver coloured light. I am not afraid.

Q: How does it feel now?

A: The tightness is less. So is the pain.

Q: So, should we move on?

A: Yes.

Q: How does the rest of the abdomen feel?

A: There is a tightness below the navel. The whole lower abdomen is tight.

Q: And the legs—the thighs, the calves, the ankles?

A: The right leg is very different from the left. There is a lot of pain here. A lot of tight pain on the outer side of the right thigh. The knee feels very weak. There is no feeling in the right ankle.

The left leg feels okay.

Q: And the feet?

A: I can barely feel the feet.

Q: So where would you like to be?

A: At the solar plexus. I would like to explore this cord. Why is there this hole?

Q: So let us 'Be' there.

(A long silence in which the person feels and senses this area.)

A: Ah, I know who this is. It is my mother. I am very attached to her. I take her pain.

Q: So how is this area now?

A: There is a lot of lightness now. No pain, no tension, it feels very free. The whole body is energized!

Q: Look above the head. What do you see?

A: Golden... a golden halo...

Q: Inside the head?

A: Sparkles. It feels very light. The pain in the centre is also much better. The right and left sides of the head are now balanced.

Q: Neck?

A: Light... no tension. Inside the neck, the head, the chest, there is the flow of a very soft, liquid energy.

Q: Chest?

A: Happy... pink... droplets of gold...

Q: Abdomen?

A: Block of PEACE.

Q: Look at the whole and just be with it.

(Pause while he feels the whole being.)

A: The whole body feels well now. I also feel quietness inside and a lightness. There is a flow of light from the top of the head to the feet. The feet are fully alive now. They were releasing pain in the beginning but now they are well. There is still a little stiffness in the outer side of the right thigh but on the whole it feels good. I am going to open the eyes now.

END NOTE

This is what happens when we are not trying to get rid of a problem. When you try to remove a problem by healing, you only put a balm or a bandage on it. But when you truly feel, sense and try to understand it, the light flows spontaneously. You don't have to call it or visualise it, it is there. The light is there within you, so there is no fear. In every human being there is this light. The moment you stand within, this light is seen. You cannot prevent it. But when you try to pull the light, you create something artificial, so you feel vulnerable again.

This experience of light, peace or joy will be there again and again in the inner spaces. When you stand in the shadows without shrinking, this light will always come to the surface. Slowly then, you can acknowledge yourself. Wherever you are, inside yourself or out in the world with others, you bring this quality with yourself irrespective of the situation. We exist because of this presence. (See Appendix II.)

As Sri Aurobindo writes, "Who indeed could dare enjoy that which is devoid of bliss? He only could dare it who is all-blissful. As for him who is devoid of bliss, he while enjoying the blissless, would still not enjoy it, would rather perish without bliss. Who can become weak? He only can who is all-powerful. The weak one indeed invaded by weakness would not endure, but would perish without force. Who could enter Ignorance? Only He who is omniscient could enter it. As for the ignorant, he could not endure in that darkness, non-being would remain non-being only. It would perish without knowledge. Ignorance is the play of knowledge, concealing itself in itself. Weakness is the play of power, blisslessness is the play of bliss, the concealment of itself in itself...

Ignorance is the root of this idea that I am but finite and therefore incapable, weak and sorrowful. I have to act, know and achieve with labour, at the expense of energy, incurring mortality. Thou art that, I am this, that which thou art I am not, that which is good for thee is bad for me, I lose by that by which thou gainest, I shall be happy only if I kill thee. I am not at all so illumined and happy that I may make thee happy by my own suffering, by my own loss and by my death, etc. This is the form of Ignorance in Mind."*

* *Sri Aurobindo. Sriaravindupanishad. Pondicherry; Sri Aurobindo Ashram Trust, 2000, pp. 27–29.*

SUMMARY

1. In the inner work, it is *important* to steadily and patiently view all with understanding—the pleasant and the unpleasant.

2. The acceptance of both, the pleasant and the unpleasant, is itself a freedom.

3. This freedom allows us to go into areas which we have avoided looking at and which are a source of disequilibrium in us.

4. Just patiently waiting with awareness and a wish to understand the cause of 'my' suffering helps to reveal the problem.

5. Standing without flinching, in front of the problem, allows the source to reveal itself.

6. It is important to do as much as one can at a time. This session created a shift. More will be done. There is never any failure, only steps in awareness.

7. It is important to know that sometimes shifts occur without any mental understanding or images. The process is not logical.

An inner imagery

For some people images come naturally. These people are gifted with imagination and an ability to create. If they are conscious, they can manifest what they see. However, many of us due to an emphasis on analytic ways of thinking may lose this gift. This does not prevent us from looking inside and healing the body. In fact as we go on exploring the inner spaces, images start coming back to us.

It is important to realize that all images do not connect to what is happening physically. For healing the physical body, sensations which arise in the physical are more reliable.

Since we are made of many layers, images can come from any layer. They can also come from beyond our self, from the universe around, below or above. The process then goes into the domain of yoga or mysticism and not of healing the body, though of course it can be used sometimes for this purpose also.

The person below is a designer, to whom images come naturally. The passage is an extract from her full healing process that spanned a few months. After looking deeply and across lifetimes, she healed herself of many chronic problems.

D: In the last three days I have developed a very severe headache. My nerves are very painful and yesterday I had to go to sleep at 12 noon. When I woke up my head was aching. By the time I got up and went to have tea, my whole body was also aching. Now I feel very weak. There is still pain in the head that feels like a bar of steel. When I am meditating, if the force comes here, it causes a lot of pain.

V: Do you feel capable of looking inside today?

D: I can try. If I don't manage you can do healing for me.

V: So we start on the journey inside. We start by feeling Her Presence with us.

(Pause)

Now we look above the head, inside the head and around the body.

D: I feel like a pressure above the head. It is like a thick mass.

V: And around the body?

D: Everything is getting pulled down. There is a grey thing coming out.

V: What does it look like?

D: Like a cloud... all over... a cloud that has a thick mass.

V: Is it filled with water?

D: It is a substance in itself... sand? Something like that.

V: Dry?

D: Yes.

V: As you say that, what happens?

D: I can see the granules falling.

V: And what is the effect?

D: They have become thick.

V: How is the head?

D: It is also filled with this thick mass. There is a hole in the centre. It has light. It is steel grey. It is very old, chipped and raw. There are raw edges so it pains everywhere. It is heavy. I feel it like a huge mountain. It is blocking every-thing.

V: Then we come to the eyes, how do they feel?

D: They feel very tight. I just want to close them.

V: Then we come to the throat.

D: It is dusty and itchy.

V: Is it like when one wants to cry but cannot?

D: It is an irritation, an anger...

V: Which cannot be expressed?

D: Yes!

V: Then we come to the chest.

D: It feels very heavy now. The whole thing is sinking here. It is a feeling of oppression. I want to just let loose.

V: And what are the colours?

D: All greyish...

V: Then we come to the abdomen.

D: It feels as if it is dead. It is sucking inside. It is like when a tyre is punctured, that's what it feels like inside.

V: Next we come to the pelvis.

D: Pain... there is a lot of pain... the thighs are aching, the knees are really weak, the legs are very, very weak.

V: Now look at the whole together. How much of you does this mess occupy?

D: Everything. It is like a rag doll... a puppet. I am just hanging like that... an iron on top, like a finger... holding it... I am like loose and helpless.

V: Can you see the finger that is holding it?

D: It is like a hand.

V: Whose hand is it?

D: It is a machine-like hand.

V: What does it represent?

D: Control over this rag-like thing.

V: Who is controlling this rag doll?

D: There is a monster.

V: Who is the monster?

D: I do not know why but I am getting images of my mother. I am getting a very uneasy feeling.

V: When you say that, what happens?

D: Guilt arises. The monster is now looking at me. It is loosening its grip and shrinking in size. It is going on looking at me. It is afraid that I have recognized it. It is shrinking. It was itself weak and needed me to nourish it. It is scared. There is air coming out of this huge skin-coloured being. It has become like a mouse.

V: Just BE with the monster. BE with the monster and watch it. It is not that you want it dead but you deeply understand it.

D: The monster wants to cry. He is very lonely, very lonely, very scared. Actually I am wondering how I could ever be scared of it. It needs the rag doll. The monster is clinging to the rag doll. It knows that it has been recognised, been seen. It is sitting down; it is scared, it has left the doll and is alone. It is hiding its face in its hands and crying loudly. It is releasing. Now it can cry. That is such a relief. Now the rag doll has seen this monster but is too tired to do anything. It is just lying fearlessly now. It is feeling compassion for the monster. The monster is incapable of doing harm. It is very unhappy, very sad. The monster has been very hurt. It is hurt.

V: What could heal the monster?

D: Love. Love from the rag doll.

V: Love from everything. Can the monster open to the vibration of love?

D: The monster is leaving now. It is very tired. It is resting now... very, very tired. It is lying down to sleep... a peaceful sleep. The doll has now got up. It has removed the chain and gently put it down. It is walking. It is free. No attachment to the monster. It is moving away from the past to the light.

V: Can you be with the doll and see what happens?

D: The doll is walking in a sky-like thing, there is a path of white clouds. It is walking on it. There is a very pleasant feel about it. It has completely forgotten about the monster and left it behind. The sun is in front. It is walking towards it. It has gone into the light. It is bathing in the light. All the dirt and stress is coming out. It is like a phoenix.

V: To expand... to be free...

D: The body is getting hot.

V: Is it unbearable?

D: I can feel it.

V: How is the abdomen now?

D: It is in the head. In the head the heat is too much.

V: What about that block?

D: I cannot feel it.

V: How is the band around the head?

D: The awareness is there, otherwise it has passed. The headache is not there anymore.

V: How are the eyes?

D: They feel very light.

V: How is the throat?

D: All right.

V: Again to the abdomen... how does it feel?

D: It doesn't feel sunk anymore. It is back into place.

V: How is the base of the spine?

D: Energy...

V: Hip?

D: Okay.

V: How is the thigh? Is it still weak? Does it pain?

D: A little bit when I touch here. A little spongy feeling. I feel good except for this heat.

V: Can you allow this warmth to expand?

D: Yes... it is going into my aura. Golden with a white outline. I am on the surface. Bonds are there... like a pressure... golden...

V: How does it feel now?

D: Overall very light but suddenly an irritation has come out.

V: How deep does it go?

D: Very deep... dark.

V: What is the colour?

D: Purple, dark deep colours, burgundy, black, dark blue, deep blue, purple, has come out. A black nozzle pipe... like this... and it's very irritated. It's like when you snap somebody out of sleep, it's like that. And as the thing sees light it is very irritated. It's not like a machine at all. It's almost like a coiled snake... hissing.

V: What energy is this?

D: It has a lot of energy; it's not a dead thing. It has a lot of energy. It has dynamism. It has the energy to kill. It's a part of me which is sadistic. It has the energy to destroy, to hurt, to kill, to give pain. It has got up now. It's hissing.

V: What creates it?

D: It seems to be its nature.

V: But what creates it? In the being where does it rest? Where does it originate?

D: It originates from the base, goes up like this, and I think it's here *(in the abdomen)*. It's resting. Its origin is here like a coil and it is putting its head on this base, sleeping like this. I think right now it doesn't want to fight. It wants to go away and shrink in a hole. Because the light is over-bearing, so it has decided... like when you wake somebody up and they don't want to fight, they just want to go away and sleep in the hole. So the energy is sleeping.

V: But try to follow it.

D: It's gone into the hole.

V: It's gone already? Can you follow it into the hole? Can you see the hole?

D: I am following.

V: Just be there and try to understand it.

D: It's now looking at me with its sharp eyes. And it's very confused. It's wondering what am I doing and why am I doing this to it. It has no intention of hurting me, it just wants to be left alone. It's not even hissing at me. It's just staring at me.

V: Try to understand...

D: It's putting its head down to rest but it's very uneasy that I am watching it. So in a very irritated manner it's watching me and putting its head up. It's tired and it's fed up. It is almost sad and saying, "Go away and leave me alone".

V: What do you want to do to it?

D: I want to hold it. I'm not afraid of it.

V: And then do what?

D: Study it and see what it is... see it.

V: Look at it.

D: Actually, I am holding it now. It's closing its eyes. It is sad. It wants to be understood. It is really tired of wanting to be understood. It is hugging me. It is on my neck. It's come out. It's around my legs. It's recognizing me. It's getting friendlier. And now it's gone and sat in the pond. It's calling me. It's trapped.

V: What traps it?

D: The darkness. It doesn't know a way out. It's always been in the darkness. It's very unhappy in the darkness. It's chained, actually emotionally chained. It's saying, it has been made to stay here, but it doesn't want to.

V: Can you make it free?

D: I think I can. I have held it. And I am bringing it out of the tunnel and I am bringing it to the light. It's really enjoying the light now and it's feeling very secure, rejuvenated and fresh. It has dissolved. It's gone. It's gone.

V: Can you still see the hole? Is it there or is it gone?

D: It's ending now. So I can open it like this. I have cleaned it with golden light. It is still like steel. It will not dissolve so easily.

V: But then you don't have to dissolve the hole, you can just be with it.

D: I have opened it a little bit, the metal marks are still there but I have touched it with gold. And it's still there... it is still black.

V: Just BE there. Be with the hole and see what happens as you are there, just be.

D: It's an open hole.

V: Just be there.

D: There are many snakes peeping out with amusement. And they are like prisoners, like prisoners seeing one of them escape. They are talking to each other... with respect for me, and looking up to me with awe. I can see a little bit of hope in them. They are trapped. Slowly some are coming out, crawling. They are bleeding from it. My structure is rising. It's very huge, it's light and the droplets are falling on everything. They are like polished cannonballs... that's the feeling. The snakes were punished... in that form... and now they all just want to dissolve. So now I see just a golden area.

V: What about the hole?

D: It's not there, it's a golden area. Because I am too huge. Everything is now gold. Everything is a cylinder, spreading out sideways. Now there is no separation, it is all gold.

END NOTE

1. Despite the vivid imagery and the many revelations, the healing is not yet complete.

2. At the same time, these images helped her to SEE the inner and outer space effortlessly.

3. The tendency to try and make things well became a hindrance.

4. Each of these images could be interpreted by people specializing in psychology but we do not do so. We let the images speak to the person itself. The mental understanding is secondary to the experience. It is the experience that has the power to heal.

The resistance to inner work

When we look inside at an area that is suffering, some-times it is not so easy. The first problem many people en-counter, is: "Will I be able to connect?" "Will I be able to see anything?" And the discovery that we CAN is reward-ing in itself. Apart from people who are too intellectual or trained to analyse everything almost all of us can feel or see.

The next challenge is NOT to want only the pleasant and get rid of the unpleasant. There comes also the hab-it of constantly judging and framing our experience. The UNDERSTANDING of the suffering relieves it automatic-ally. There is no effort involved to try and improve things. We are perfect in our essence. The work is to let our essence take over!

Once we are inside, there can come an unwillingness to look deeper or a feeling that "I must open my eyes now". In such cases we have to let the inner being guide us. If we cannot trust ourselves yet, it is good to have a sensitive person guide us from outside.

In the case of chronic problems, we may not get instan-taneous results. This happens because the roots of the problem we are looking at are too deep or too complex. Then we must patiently practice day after day till the inner depths bring the roots to the surface.

And sometimes, it is the natural tendency of inertia, a heaviness that takes over. The case below is a study of one of the ways the resistance comes and how to get over it.

S: This mud is tiring me. It is pulling me down... just eating me.

V: Does it remind you of something?

S: I don't know... yes... my mother. It is giving me that feeling. Of my mother dominating me... yes... that is the feeling that is coming. I am totally getting squashed. I have no brain and I have no space... it's actually an experience of domination... helpless actually... tamed by events. It's actually a karmic pattern*. It comes back every five or ten years. It could be work environment, relationship or whatever. This is that experience. When I get dominated by the external darkness, helplessness, sadness, depression... it is the depression of the other person that enters into me. It is the darkness, helplessness, sadness, depression of an external force that gets into me and I don't have the power to reject it. Yes, this is it. It started with my mother and later it was in work, friendships, relationships. This is that karmic pattern. A very strong karmic pattern.

V: What allows it to enter you?

S: Actually I don't want it to enter me. But I don't have the

* Patterns from the soul's past actions

power to throw it out, because it doesn't belong to me. It has entered into me and is holding me down and I don't have the strength to push it back now, and to be away from this darkness.

Now I am this light. I am getting up now. There is this huge boulder that I am pushing and pushing and pushing; it's on the side now. It is on the side and I am here. The form of light is increasing and increasing.

V: Can you go into the boulder?

S: The boulder? I am now higher than the sun. I am now not afraid of the boulder. Maybe now I can pick it up.

(Long pause in which she looks at the scene inside)

Can I speak? So now I am as large as the sun. So now, for me, it doesn't make a difference. I have picked it up and put it in the heart. Though I let it melt there is no empathy for the boulder.

V: Can you enter into the boulder?

S: But why? Because now I am very huge and I am not fearing that boulder.

V: You would like it to disappear? *(Laughs because the person automatically would like the problem to disappear)*

S: Yes. It is disappearing. I have no sympathy with the boulder and no empathy.

V: It's not an emotion... it is like the whole and no part is excluded from the whole. You do not throw anything out. Everything belongs to you and this is also there... it is accepted. There is an acceptance.

S: I have taken it and it has dissolved inside me but I didn't have any emotion. It doesn't exist now. There was no emotion. I just picked it up and dissolved it, so... it's gone. In a positive way it is gone.

V: How do you feel now?

S: I still feel that huge being of light.... I feel like a nice giant... not powerful... just relishing the beauty of being so huge. I am just getting bigger and bigger. Now I see gold everywhere.

V: How do you feel?

S: It's okay. I don't feel any depression. From the lower part of the body that sort of anxiety has gone. A little physical pain is there in the feet. There is an irritation. Something has woken up. As I looked at the foot something has awakened that was sleeping. A huge python and it is under a tree, like in a desert, it is green and brown in colour with black spots. It's coiled and its head is like this. It's not doing anything. It wants to stop this journey inside. Actually I am very tired. I can't journey anymore.

V: What does this represent, this python?

S: Yeah! It is inertia. Yes, it is inertia. It has exactly that feeling. I don't want to do the inner work anymore.

V: What is the python doing now?

S: It is very irritated now. My mind is very irritated. Anger is coming that I am not stopping the looking. The python is resisting. It won't do anything. Oh God! Can't I open my eyes? I don't want to do this. I don't want to do this.

(V laughs)

What is that? It is inertia. Oh God! Inertia is part of the physical mind, right? Now what? Can we do it next time?

V: We are not doing anything. We are just understanding... we are being aware... we are just looking. Everything has a right to be there. Our way is not to throw things out or to destroy what we don't like inside us... to be pure and perfect... no... we are what we are...

S: Okay. Now the python is willing but it is very tired.

V: So just be with the tiredness. You are not trying to escape the tiredness. The tiredness exists and you are aware of it. You are experiencing it fully, without trying to get rid of it. It is like you are going into the core of tiredness.

S: Actually I want to do this. It might take a lot of time so let us do it next time.

V: We have time. At this moment it is there and we are with it. You need not close your eyes, just be aware of the feeling of tiredness.

S: You know this is it. The reason why I need to sleep so much, this is it. You know I can't work more than 10 minutes, 15 minutes. My physical might have a lot of energy, but this part, it gets tired. This is it.

V: What creates this?

S: I'll just go there. It's the heaviness of the python. It doesn't want to move. It just wants to sleep and so whenever I am full of life and want to do things, it pulls me down. This python has the power to pull me down and now it wants to sleep. It is a very sluggish sleep.

V: What is the purpose of this python?

S: I think the python has been fed with a lot of bad food which is not digested. So it is carrying in it this undigested raw material. And the poor python is helpless. It can't raise its head. Whatever is inside, it just pulls it down. I don't know what to do with that bad stuff inside.

V: There is nothing to do. Just be aware of the sense of heaviness that exists.

S: I think it is *samskara**. I do not know why that word is coming to me. It seems like a mass of samskaras that I have inherited from the past, which is the heavy mass that is inside the python.

V: How do you feel now?

S: The python feels dirty carrying the mass. It doesn't want

**Association, impression, fixed notion, habitual reaction formed by one's past.*

to carry it anymore. The python is asking for help. He feels so helpless. He is the carrier of this horrible mass.

He can shed it off. It is coming out. You know, like the snakes shed off their skin? So it is coming out. That mass inside, you know how raw uncooked meat looks like, that is how it looks like. It is foul, it is horrible, it is a dustbin. The python has taken off its skin. It has crumpled to the ground. I don't know, it might be dead. But this mass is living, this is what was giving life to the python. The python was like a dead skin, crumpled. It's like lumps of skin colour... red spots, purple spots.... It is like the drawing of a brain, sorry intestine. It is like that—it has life, it is sticky. I am trying to open it now, with courage. It is like pressing it flat. It is separating itself out. It is like a thick roti*. It is causing pain. It is a very heavy weight.

V: From where do these *samskaras* come?

S: They come from my parents, their parents and families and they don't belong to me. A detachment is there. They don't belong to me. In fact now a light is coming. I am getting lighter because I have put it out. I see what was being carried. I see an ocean wave coming and I want to dissolve all in it now. I carry that weight and I take it to the ocean. The waves are coming to help me to dissolve it. I have put it softly in the ocean. It's floating like this... down. There is a huge mass that has rested on the bedrock. It is dissolving slowly in the water.

V: How do you feel the air? Look around....

*A type of Indian bread.

S: Oh, it's a beach, an island.

V: What is happening in the air?

S: That is clean now. The samskaras are dissolving. I am in a beautiful environment. The tree is still there. That is shady. There is a sun. There is clean wide air. Blue water... there is a little green colour below. It is very shallow. It is a very alive place. I can feel the freshness of the waves. It is very lively, full of life.

V: How do you feel?

S: I am free outside. I am not afraid of the samskaras. I am in a very straight posture under the tree. I am just a skin-coloured silhouette... pinkish, light brown.

V: How do you feel?

S: When I look at my face, it is you know, like a *neelam* stone. It is inside, here... purplish, bluish.

V: How do you feel?

S: I feel wonderful. Now there is another stone here. A topaz, a huge, real topaz, red coloured. My legs are green. I am blowy, like a leaf. Now I am twirling. I have lain down on the beach. The wind is blowing. There is the total experience of freedom and light. A darkness has come. This has come suddenly. It is a tension that doesn't want me to be free.

V: What is it that does not want to be free?

S: The past.

V: What in the past?

S: Chains. Linkages.

V: Why?

S: It wants me to be stressful. It feels that life is not meant to be free. Life is meant to have mountains of stress and I can see a door that is waiting for me to come back into all the compartments again. That is where these chains, these strings are coming from. It is now a thin silver wire which is just pulling me into that. But I am taking it off. I let it go. Now for the first time I am feeling ungripped here. I have taken a decision to let it go.

The falsehood of that place has dissolved now. It only exists if I agree to come back. It was a falsehood in the first place. The python has cracked now. It has crumpled and dissolved. The sun is there, the sands are there, the water is clean and flowing. A new me is washing its face in the water. Now I have a human body. I have taken a human form. I am just on the beach, twirling...

(Opens her eyes)

So what happened?

V: How do you feel?

S: I feel I actually saw the *samskaras*, the python, because the inertia that was gripping me is the root cause of a lot of things. They were marks from the past in my brain which have to be flattened. It was a dead mass. But from where did they come?

V: I don't give such answers. You have to look within for it when you really want to.

S: But what have we done? This mass, this...

V: We have done a tremendous amount of work today.

S: Yeah! Very true... a lot of work mentally.

V: It's not mental, it's from the inner consciousness. You have worked to free yourself.

S: Yeah, I did.

V: You put a lot of energy to free yourself, to be with the problem, to see it. You shifted from the subtle into the physical. It's more concrete now.

S: Oh, that's why the physical form...

V: So we will continue this work of being aware.

END NOTE

It is interesting to note the spontaneous tendency to get rid of what is troubling us. In the inner healing process, this tendency becomes a barrier to going deeper. By giving mental explanations to an experience that was unpleasant, we feel relieved. But this relief is only temporary. The problem will come back. So there will be more opportunities to look again!

Another interesting thing in this session was the image of the boulder which was dissolved, turning into a python when pushed to continue the process. It is like the inner being of S knew that the problem was not gone and showed her the same problem in another way. This creativity that we all have is impressive.

The only way when facing this inertia, this unwillingness to go on, is to know you have to go on, today or tomorrow...

As long as we are on this earth, we will be in movement. Nothing is static, nothing is as we imagine it should be. It is what it is. As we accept our self, we can change. This is the greatest revelation.

The Journey

Once this way of connecting to the body becomes spontaneous, the fear of illness can decrease. Whenever something is not at ease, one can look inside, connect and the difficulty is resolved as the light, peace, joy or presence enter. At no time should one judge oneself for not being able to connect or resolve a problem. The wisdom to seek help by other ways is also needed at times.

This way can be used along with other forms of treatment. It awakes and strengthens us in all ways. Inner vision and sense grow and blossom. We find ourselves more in peace and harmony with our nature.

The body is our base in this work. People with a natural inclination to enter subtle worlds can find themselves drifting. It is important for them to constantly check with the body sensations. Inner experiences will have no concrete result without this anchor.

It is also important to realise that the inner worlds are like the ocean. There are many layers and zones. Here we are using the simple link between the soul and body. Other domains are the realm of occultism or Yoga.

Past-life experiences, Karmic insights, insights from the womb, connections to spirit guides or gurus can happen along with other not so pleasant things. Keeping a neutral, non-reacting attitude and contact with the body is essential. In case one has a tendency to enter these spaces, it is better not to do this work alone.

When two people concentrate together, the way becomes easier and the focus most often intense. So one person can question (intuitively, only when needed) and the other person looks and expresses what is happening.

This work is a journey through the body that can be undertaken anytime, anywhere.

The human body is special. It contains all the earth's past evolutionary history. It is now tuning itself to a profound shift where it will spontaneously be connected to the Truth/God, where its matter itself will be made of knowledge rather than ignorance and inertia. Then of course disease will be a thing of the past and old age and death disappear!

Appendices

The passages in the appendices are extracts from the words of the Mother and Sri Aurobindo. They are the Yogic base of this way of healing.

Appendix I describes the principle on which this book is founded.

Appendix II is an extract from the Mother's own experience of the physical mind's role in creating suffering and detachment from it as the cure for physical illness.

APPENDIX I

"Our surface cognition, our limited and restricted mental way of looking at our self, at our inner movements and at the world outside us and its objects and happenings, is so constituted that it derives in different degrees from a four-fold order of knowledge.

The original and fundamental way of knowing, native to the occult self in things, is a knowledge by identity; the second, derivative, is a knowledge by direct contact associated at its roots with a secret knowledge by identity or starting from it, but actually separated from its source and therefore powerful but incomplete in its cognition; the third is a knowledge by separation from the object of observation, but still with a direct contact as its support or even a partial identity; the fourth is a completely separative knowledge which relies on a machinery of indirect contact, a knowledge by acquisition which is yet, without being conscious of it, a rendering or bringing up of the contents of a pre-existent inner awareness and knowledge. A knowledge by identity, a knowledge by intimate direct contact, a knowledge by separative direct contact, a wholly separative knowledge by indirect contact, are the four cognitive methods of Nature.

The first way of knowing in its purest form is illustrated in the surface mind only by our direct awareness of our own essential existence: it is a knowledge empty of any other content than the pure fact of self and being; of nothing else in the world has our surface mind the same kind of awareness. But in the knowledge of the structure and movements of our subjective consciousness some element of awareness by identity does enter; for we can project ourselves with a certain identification into these movements. It has already been noted how this can happen in the case of an uprush of wrath which swallows us up so that for the moment our whole consciousness seems to be a wave of anger: other passions, love, grief, joy have the same power to seize and occupy us; thought also absorbs and occupies, we lose sight of the thinker and become the thought and the thinking. But very ordinarily there is a double movement; a part of our selves becomes the thought or the passion, another part of us either accompanies it with a certain adherence or follows it closely and knows it by an intimate direct contact which falls short of identification or entire self-oblivion in the movement. ... we can detach ourselves, separate the being from its temporary becoming, observe it, control it, sanction or prevent its manifestation: we can, in this way, by an inner detachment, a mental or spiritual separateness, partially or even fundamentally liberate ourselves from the control of mind nature or vital nature over the being and assume the position of the witness, knower and ruler. Thus we have a double knowledge of the subjective movement: there is an intimate knowledge, by identity, of its stuff and its force of action, more intimate than we could have by any entirely separative and objective knowledge such as we get of things outside us, things that are to us altogether not-self; there is at the same time a knowledge by detached observation, detached but with a power of direct contact, which frees us from engrossment by the Nature-energy and enables us to relate the movement to the rest of our own existence and world existence. If we are without this detachment, we lose our self of being and mastering knowledge in the nature self of becoming and movement and action and, though we know intimately the movement, we do not know it dominatingly and fully. This would not be the case if we carried into our identification with the movement our identity with the rest of our subjective existence,— if, that is to say, we could plunge wholly into the wave of becoming and at the same time be in the very absorption of the state or act the mental witness, observer, controller; but this we cannot easily do, because we live in a divided consciousness in which the vital part of us,—our life nature of force and desire and passion and action,—tends to control or swallow up the mind, and the mind has to avoid this subjection and control the vital, but can only succeed in the effort by keeping itself separate; for if it identifies itself, it is lost and hurried away in the life movement. Nevertheless a kind of balanced double identity by division is possible, though it is not easy to keep the balance; there is a self of thought which observes and permits the passion for the sake of the experience,—or is obliged by some life-stress to permit it,—and there is a self of life which allows itself to be carried along in the movement of Nature. Here, then, in our subjective experience, we have a field of the action of consciousness in which three movements of cognition can meet together, a certain kind of knowledge by identity, a knowledge by direct contact and, dependent upon them, a separative knowledge."

Sri Aurobindo, The Life Divine. Sri Aurobindo Ashram Trust, Pondicherry, 1970, pp. 524–26.

APPENDIX II

"Suffering also comes through the physical mind, because if this entity is calmed down, we no longer suffer—exactly what happened to me!

The physical mind, you see, makes use of the nervous substance; if we withdraw it from the nervous substance, we no longer feel anything, for that's what gives us the perception of sensation.... We know something is wrong, but we no longer suffer from it.

This was a very important experience. Afterwards (especially yesterday afternoon and this morning), I gradually began to realise that this kind of indifferent detachment is the ESSENTIAL condition for the establishment of true Harmony in the most material Matter—the most external, physical Matter (Mother pinches the skin of her hand).

This experience has been like a stage—an indispensable stage for establishing this complete detachment; an indispensable stage so that the harmony of the body-consciousness (which came with the body's experience of the Divine) might have its effect upon the most external, superficial part of the body.

This is the logical consequence of the research I have been doing for a long time now on the cause of illnesses and how to overcome them."

The Mother, Agenda: Vol. II. Mira Trust, Paris, 1961, p. 53.

Pain brings us back to a deeper truth by obliging us to concentrate in order to be able to bear it, be able to face this thing that crushes us...The secret is to emerge from the ego, get out of its prison, unite ourselves with the Divine, merge into Him, not to allow anything to separate us from Him. Then, once one has discovered this secret and realises it in one's being, pain loses its justification and suffering disappears. It is an all-powerful remedy, not only in the deeper parts of the being, in the soul, in the spiritual consciousness, but also in life and in the body.

There is no illness, no disorder which can resist the discovery of this secret and the putting of it into practice, not only in the higher parts of the being but in the cells of the body.

The Mother, Questions and Answers – 1957–1958.
Sri Aurobindo Ashram Trust, Pondicherry, 2003, pp. 41–43

Absolute cure of an illness so that it cannot return again depends on clearing the mind, the vital and body consciousness of the psychological response to the Force bringing the illness.... The complete immunity from all illness for which our yoga tries can only come by a total and permanent enlightenment of the below from above resulting in the removal of the psychological roots of ill health – it cannot be done otherwise.

Sri Aurobindo, Letters on Yoga: Vol. 24. Sri Aurobindo Ashram Trust, Pondicherry, 1970, p. 1571.